ISBN: 978-1-66783-653-9

WE THREE

Written and Illustrated by
Holly Brookman

Here is where this story begins,

with the billowing blue face of the North Wind.

She, of far reaching and far roaming eyes,

scattering the seeds of change into the skies.

And so unfolds this unusual tale,

about three individuals who learn to prevail.

The first one we meet was abruptly blown

into a far away land where she was gently sown.

The yellow sun and rain doing their best,

nurturing the dormant soul quietly at rest.

Along came a beautiful spring day,

and a flower sprang up from the ground and

said "Hey! My name is Penelope. Would you like to play?"

The other flowers she smiled at deeply frowned.

Penelope could not understand why they refused to turn 'round.

"Well," they explained, "You're so ungainly, so much taller than us.

You really don't belong, and that you can trust."

This was how it went, day after day. Penelope tried so

hard, but their opinions would not be swayed.

One night as Penelope slept under the full moon,

she awoke hearing enchanting whispers dancing upon a tune.

"One day your life will be just right. Know you will be happy,

and you will take flight."

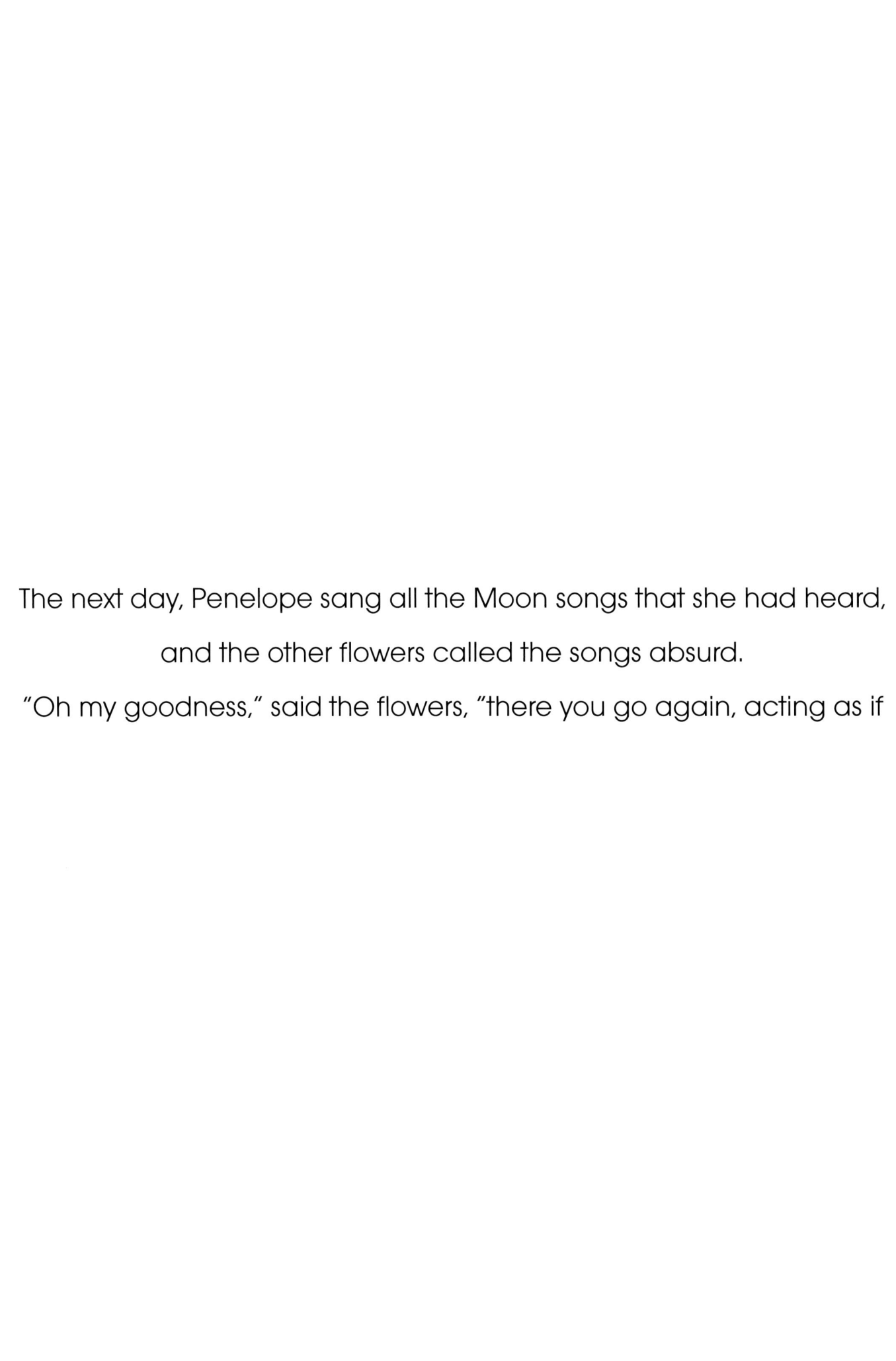

The next day, Penelope sang all the Moon songs that she had heard,
and the other flowers called the songs absurd.
"Oh my goodness," said the flowers, "there you go again, acting as if

the Moon is your friend!"

"The only thing that will ever be flying free, is your imagination about

things that can't be!"

As their petals were fluttering and this conversation took place,

someone began listening and slowing her pace.

The flowers conversation she had plainly heard, even though

no one else reacted to their words.

She felt admiration and sympathy,

for this sad flower wanting to be free.

The girl smiled at Penelope and revealed,

"Our troubles are similar and our ordeals,

As the two pondered this state of affairs,

they realized some are jealous of panache

And bright flair!

Penelope said "Do you know the Moon was

my first friend,

And she told me a tale of three that would ascend..."

The little girl smiled knowingly and their friendship had begun,

Two kindred spirits waiting for one.

That night the Moon began floating in the violet sky,

singing a song and coaxing the sand from our eyes.

The Moon's rippling light created a path,

upon which Penelope and the girl did latch.

Before you could say "Hey Diddle Dee,

The girl and Penelope flew into a land that

made three.

Where did the moonbeams take the two? Suddenly,

they found themselves at a dark and forbidding zoo.

The girl and her flower friend looked way up high,

Seeing an ancient wrinkled face that was starting to cry.

The girl and Penelope walked over to meet

an old elephant with flat and rounded feet.

This was Rumbles of great height, his brown eyes

twinkling and bright.

His grey skin showing the signs of much wear, with deep lines

Undulating every here and every there.

While his trunk waved sadly in the air,

He began his sad story with the utmost of care.

"When I was young, with my mother by my side,

we would build mud mountains,

on which we all would slide.

Up early in the morning with the birds and the sun,

our antics starting after the day had begun.

After the long day ended and we were wiped out,

The Sun and clouds would soon start to pout.

A banner of stars unfurling into the dark night,

Watching over our herd, sleeping so close and so tight.

Until one awful day, strange people came and stole me away!

My brave mother, to protect me, did her best,

But there was a thunderous boom forcing

her to rest.

My sweet mother, turning slowly around,

called out my name when she fell to the ground.

"Rumbles, my darling" she said speaking softly to me,

"I promise I will see you again at the lions throne by the

baobab tree."

My tears were forever to stream,

because my mother only exists in my dreams.

Then the hunters wrapped me with heavy steel chains

Forcing me into the box car of a dark train.

And so I was stolen at this tender age,

Spending the rest of my life in ropes and a cage.

Strangers would come and toss me some hay

And I began to work, never again allowed to play.

The strangers would beat me to perform silly tricks,

Urging me on with sharp jabs and hard kicks.

This went on endlessly for so many years,

Now my broken body can only make tears.

And there are no more silly tricks for me,

I stay at this zoo and standing under this tree.

Last night, I dreamt of my Mother

and wondered what to do.

In my dream she said "Rumbles your troubles

will soon be through."

The little girl who was crying, wiped her eyes on her sleeve,

Sensed that time was pressing and Rumbles' must leave.

Speaking earnestly in front of the other two,

"We must get Rumbles out of this zoo!

We three just want to be happy and free.

We must escort Rumbles back to his family."

Penelope opened her eyes and mouth wide with shock,

"How will we all get there? Will we just walk?

"Africa is a long way off, we need to talk!"

The little girl said "Penelope, please don't say we can't,

Remember how you felt when the

other flowers told you that?"

Suddenly, the Moon's big eyes

began to blink,

and lavender moon dust did murmur and speak.

The zoo was so silent, all the other animals asleep,

and into Rumbles enclosure moonbeams did creep.

Rumbles saw sparkling lights dancing around his feet,

"I think this is happening now, and not next week!"

The moonbeams magic powers gently did nudge,

lifting the big elephant into the night sky above.

The lavender dust caused Rumbles to sway to and fro,

The two others gasping, were gently swept up in tow.

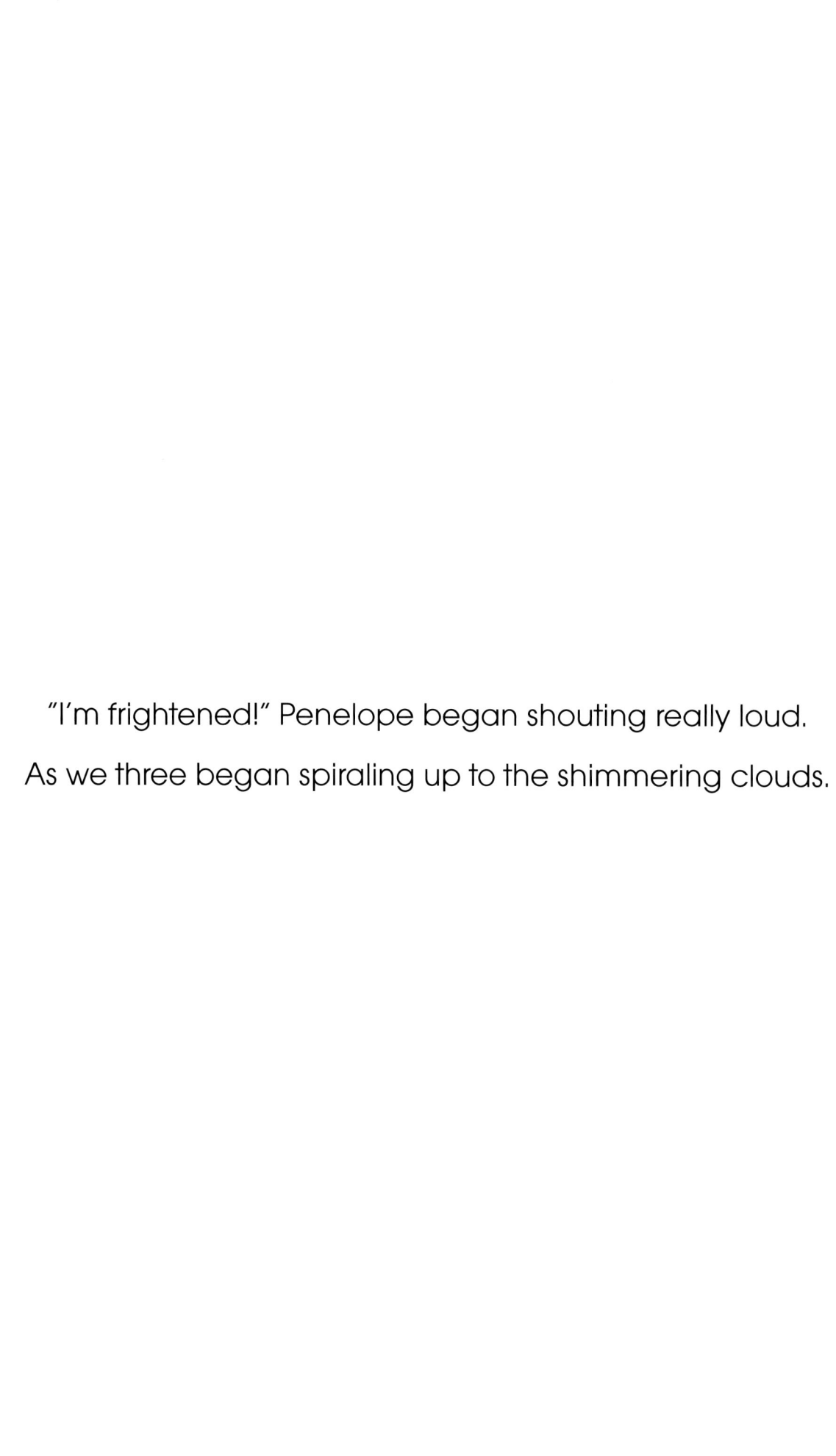

"I'm frightened!" Penelope began shouting really loud.

As we three began spiraling up to the shimmering clouds.

Flying is such an exhilarating thing!

Soaring above any troubles that life sometimes brings.

All the trees waving riotously "Hello"

from hundreds of feet far down below.

The little girl laughing , as the wind brushed her face,

"We three decide which way we go,

with the gentle night breeze showing us so."

Suddenly an uneasy crowd gathered below,

A group of uneasy people who did not know

What we three were about and where we would go.

They shouted at us loudly to come down to the ground,

Hurling sharp spears to make us crash down.

"Rumbles and Penelope" the girl called to her friends,

"We're in grave danger, our odyssey might end!"

Rumbles looking around, his eyes wide with fear,

Was doing his best to help them dodge all the spears.

Then Penelope said, "I know what to do!"

"Lets ask for the help of you know who!"

"Moon, Moon, Your help is needed please!"

And beautiful Luna responded with a

tremendous sneeze.

Before you could say, "Hey, I can't see," moon-dust

surrounded we three.

Hiding us safely from the danger below,

our little procession continued merrily in tow,

Gliding over the rolling seas and ground,

the moonbeams guided us safely down.

Where were we now, and what should we do?

We three stared at each other for some type of clue.

"My foggy old brain doesn't remember the way"

The elephant said as his ears thoughtfully swayed.

Rumbles brown eyes began welling with tears,

And Penelope did her best to calm all his fears.

"Rumbles, think back in time to the words your mother

put in your ears,

Say the words out loud so we all can hear"

" 'Rumbles', she called out to me,

'Remember the lions throne by the baobab trees'"

Beneath the branches of a distant tree we were shown

The shape of an impending stone throne.

We three began running happily down the path,

Until we heard a roar of great wrath.

A magnificent large lion, curious was he,

marching up on his massive paws towards we three.

Penelope tentatively stepped forward and with a bow,

Impressed the great lion who unfurled his brow.

"We have travelled far from across the sea,

To reunite our elephant friend with his family."

The lion then leapt upon the throne of great height,

saying "The Moon did tell me of three who took flight.

"Look to the West as the fiery sun does set.

And the Moon takes the stage, your good friend I have met."

The sun slowly retreated in a red and orange show,

As a beautiful garden around them did grow.

Then Rumbles sensitive ears heard trumpeting

and padded feet,

of familiar elephants running towards him to greet!

Their trunks were waving high in the air,

And Rumbles saw his mother returning his stare

Calling out loudly, Rumbles ran through the moonlit glow,

His mother greeting him warmly as the tears did flow.

The Elephants all cried and sang elephant songs,

And Rumbles ran to where he had always belonged.

Then the majestic lion returned Penelope's bow,

And the Moon smiled sadly as only she knows how.

Penelope and the girl knew what to do,

They stepped on the moonbeam drifting away as two.

After their long journey, through a window they did crawl.

Since nobody was looking, nobody saw.

Silently a little more did they weep.

With the Moon singing softly bringing them to sleep.

The next morning everyone in town did exclaim,

"Did you hear about last night? It was very strange!

An old elephant suddenly was gone from the zoo.

He completely vanished, as if he just flew!"

(But, we all know that can't possibly be true.)

Hearing this news an elderly grandfather in a tattered chair,

Felt a sad memory stirring somewhere,

Of his darling granddaughter and the things she did love,

Sunflowers, Elephants, and the Moon up above.

Last winter with the Moon lighting his way,

He walked outside saying what he longed to say,

Warm tears streaming from his old eyes

He opened his hand up to the Northern sky

Black and white seeds began swirling in the air,

The tiniest containers of panache and of flair.

Now you know the magic of three.

All living creatures just want to be free.

A little girl, a flower, and an old Elephant

who lost and found love.

Overcoming adversity, soaring above.

The sweet Moon who helped everyone to see.

That is quite nice, don't you agree?

The End